D0630762

MECHANICS' INSTITUTE
❦ MECHANICS' ❧
MERCANTILE LIBRARY

Zero Meridian

POEMS

Deborah Warren

WINNER OF THE NEW CRITERION POETRY PRIZE

Ivan R. Dee

CHICAGO 2004

ZERO MERIDIAN. Copyright © 2004 by Deborah Warren. All rights reserved, including the right to reproduce this book or portions thereof in any form. For information, address: Ivan R. Dee, Publisher, 1332 North Halsted Street, Chicago 60622. Manufactured in the United States of America and printed on acid-free paper.

Library of Congress Cataloging-in-Publication Data:
Warren, Deborah, 1946–
   Zero Meridian : poems / Deborah Warren.
        p. cm.
   "Winner of the New Criterion Poetry Prize."
   ISBN 1-56663-596-9 (alk. paper)
     I. Title.

PS3623.A8645Z33 2004
811'.6—dc22

2004055285

811
W287   DEC 23 2004

For my mother and father,
Margaret Turner Warren
and Howland Shaw Warren

Acknowledgments

Poems included here have appeared, or will appear, in the following publications: *Atlanta Review:* "Seeing Carthage"; *Crisis*: "Roofwalker"; *Cumberland Poetry Review*: "Aphrodite Raises Aeneas," "Iron Pants"; *Edge City Review*: "Angelica and Benedetta," "Epithets"; *Explorations*: "Closing"; *First Things*: "Domain"; *The Formalist*: "About the Rain," "Flight," "Jealousy," "Silent Reading," "The Tornado at the Door," "Regret," "Roof-Walker"; *The Hudson Review*: "The Crabapple in Flower"; *Leviathan Quarterly (UK)*: "These Same Beasts," "What the Dolphins Know"; *The New Criterion*: "A Hill"; *Pivot*: "The Tea"; *Runes*: "The Blue Dogs of Scylla"; *Slant*: "Personent hodie"; *Southern Humanities Review*: "Due Diligence"; *Southwest Review*: "Hay Field on Methodist Hill"; *The Sow's Ear*: "Happiness"; *Verse Daily*: "Roof-Walker"; *The Yale Review*: "Gibbon Motion."

Contents

I :: Silent Reading

II :: Happy, He Who Knows the Country Gods

III :: Zero Meridian

IV :: Flight

V :: The Blue Dogs of Scylla

VI :: Reading the Aeneid

VII :: Coda

Zero Meridian

I :: Silent Reading

Gibbon Motion

difficilior lectio

Look at the motion of the lucky gibbon,
pouring himself like liquid on the limb
he streams along—less animal than oil—
gliding as if there's nothing more to him
than motion. Stone-hard underneath the gibbon's
bright glissade, do aches and agonies
like mine cramp at his heart while he's sashaying
easy and elastic in the trees?

If that's the way we ought to read the gibbon,
giving him fears and headaches he suppresses,
you're like him—like me: For all your flowing
clear as water, I should look at you
guessing what's underneath your easy going
and reading you as complicated, too.

The Crabapple in Flower

The crabapple tore through the house one week in April,
boughs in armloads—room after room—in vases,
jars from the cupboards, jugs from the cellar, urns.
By what ploy did an artless flower come
—white and pink, red bud and country leaf—
laying siege to the heart of our existence?

Something to do with disparity—the flower
brief and new on the gnarled neglected branch.
And something else. The long sprays dazzled us,
but their beauty pierced us, too, with a desire
to know them, to possess them, in some way
five pale senses could never satisfy.

Anna, Emma

Anna, Emma, I turn to you—as experts
on adultery, though you're only fiction—
for advice on conducting an affair.
How to meet him, to start with. Not a ballroom;
not these days. At the office? At a bar?
How to manage the black lace, the mascara,
all the tricks that are wasted on a husband.
And I'd like a lesson in how to lie,
how to hide what will only get more flagrant
every day with the brazenness of habit.
How to handle the twinges of remorse!
And what to do when the novelty goes stale—
how to keep the romance's pages turning
faster when I can see the story's end.

Nakedness

Bathsheba washed herself beside the palace
flush with the hope of feeling David's eyes
heavy along her shoulders and her hips.
A beautiful woman always realizes
someone's watching; secretly she tenses—
Artemis, for instance, at her pond
ringed by the cypress, knew before she saw him
the soundless presence there of Actaeon.

But you're not really naked if you know
somebody could be watching. Let him stare;
you've got your wits about you for defenses.
Nakedness is being unaware:
Blanketed up to the chin, when you're asleep—
that's nakedness. The slack face in the bed,
stripped of more than clothing—it's not *there*.
And watching a sleeper in that absence is
to see through flesh and more than lay him bare.

Silent Reading

from an account by Augustine

Ambrose read silently, astonishing
those who watched and pressed around him spellbound,
never having heard of such a thing:
Romans didn't read except aloud.
And here was Ambrose who, without a sound,
swallowed the hidden words before a crowd
so thunderstruck you'd think the earth had stopped—
And twitching an instant at the poles, it had.
It leaned on its axis to read the constellations
printed in all the volumes of the sky
and shifted its shoulder, riffling the ocean's pages,
the way it does when it's stunned by something new,
and then resumed its spinning while the Romans
stood there and stared at silence, silent too.

Hay Field on Methodist Hill

From the time we cleared it, all it's been is trouble,
stubborn and recalcitrant and proud;
every winter, fractious and uncowed,
throwing up new rocks and glacier-rubble:
It's clear it never wanted to be plowed.

And once we got the stones out, it was trees
behaving as if they had the right of way:
Every March the maples have a field day
—don't expect them to give you a year of peace—
shoving, off-side, elbowing out the hay.

When the saplings get above themselves, it's over.
Let them grow a foot or so too high
and—teen-age trees? You might as well go try
and sow the sea with rocks and hope for clover,
or, if you want less trouble, plow the sky.

What the Dolphins Know

iam nostros curvi norunt delphines amores
Ovid, *Leander Heroni, Heroïdes*

Think how heavy the water was, and Sestos
far—too far to swim to every evening;
but Leander swam along a highway
blazed by habit, as if his arms, like wheels,
had beaten a liquid road in a salty thicket.
Fish, his intimates and his familiars,
sang to him, and the dolphins that dove beside him
knew the boy—all head and heel and elbow—
who grasped the sea in handfuls and pulled not water
toward his heart with his curving hands, but love.

Whether Hero forgot to light the pine-torch,
whether a hurricane tore out the fire,
whether leaping whitecaps concealed the lighthouse
doesn't matter. What I know is this:
Love is an element where thrashing strangers
bend their limbs to a medium not their own.

Maybe, if you're a lover, you're Leander
paving a path in a rolling patch of ocean.
Or you're a dolphin, beached on a stony pasture,
fins entangled in grass and ragweed—flailing—

rising—arching over the dust and pollen.
If you climb on the sky, your fingers clutching
emptiness, if your legs take hold on nothing,
then I recognize you—the way the dolphins
knew Leander, knowing it takes a lover
to race with the creatures curving through the sea.

The Tornado at the Door

I read about a gale at sea,
and the pages whirl in the printed storm.
I write, about a violent wind,
that wildness is what living's for.
And life comes pounding up to me
and stretches out its spinning arms,
and I could take the sucker in—
and every time I shut the door.

Dialogue with Myself

I spend a lot of time in haunts not only
off the beaten track—they don't exist:
Chez Swann, in Casterbridge, at Troy, at *nowhere*—

Get a life! you say. God! What you've missed!
Hey, yeah—let's spend the evening in a chair.
Let's live it up with dim protagonists.
Let's dally on the sofa with Voltaire.
It's kind of scary (not to mention lonely)
when your entire social life consists
of ghosts and venues like a blasted heath.
Besides—I have to tell you—it's escapist.
Life? Your life's a kind of living death,

you say. So do your living. As for me,
maybe I've seen some things you'll never see.

The Picture Frames at Cetinale

We left the olive trees at Ginestreto—
all around them starry in the grass
the pinpoint daisies and blue *myosotis.*
Up to the villa. Gravel walk and hedge;
up through the high *giardino a terrazze;*
inside, up again to the *salone;*
past the long dogs dozing across the sofas
and on to his collection: Picture frames.
Heavy with circumstance, their mitred arms
embraced, in fat gold, scenes by Tintoretto,
Parmigianino, Pintoricchio, others—
Titian, Veronese? I forget.

It wasn't a joke, the *picture-frame* collection.
For him the gilded rectangles surpassed
the Veroneses. Maybe he was right;
Masaccio, Lorenzetti, Duccio, Bazzi—
an embarrassment of canvases. The dogs,
as if they'd been worn out with too much beauty
—too much art—had plumped for the sofas. *He*
may have preferred the gilt frames with their *putti*
sprawled in the bosses of fat grapes. As for me,
the frames, the Titians—even more than these
I remember the things that Titian didn't paint;
the Ginestreto flowers and olive trees.

Foley Sound *

The sandals slap, the screen door slams, my sister
swishes off in a hiss of corduroys,
the cups chink in the saucers, and the morning
identifies itself with every noise:
If it's hard to get a handle on the sun
rolling inaudibly across the sky,
it's not so much its distance as its silence
that doesn't give us enough to know it by.

Show us a film where they unhook the moon
and bring it down and stake it in a field.
We won't believe our eyes. But if we hear
the creak of the ropes on the mooring pegs, then we'll
believe it—if you can convince our ears.
We'll strain to catch the wind's unwonted squeal
in the lunar craters, whether they're there or not:
It's the sound of a thing that makes it real.

* sound effects

A Hill

The net of stars that holds the night in place,
with Cassiopeia and Berenice's Hair
as fixed as a cage across the dome of space;
with Cygnus, the Lion and the Little Bear
and Taurus tame, with Orion lying there—
as long as the ground you're standing on is flat,
they're all too motionless to wonder at;

but stand on a hill, at an angle to the sky,
and it's not so much that you look them in the eye;
it's this: Orion, the Bear, the Gemini
go wheeling around an evening gone askew—
the whole horizon pitched and out of true,
the night undone and still in the making, new
and enough off balance to be dazzled by.

The Road from Aulis

Riding in on the islands' windy sea-lanes,
there they waited, delayed by onshore gales,
wasting oil and flour, bobbing there—
the captains bored with the dice and wine and boys.
And why? Because of a goddess's creature slaughtered;
there they sat for a fuss about a hare.

You (supposing your ships were stuck in Aulis),
say you got a consultant—put some Calchas
on the problem. And say his answer was
to recommend that you sacrifice your daughter:
Good solution, matched in fatuity
only by the lunacy of the cause.

Don't ask anyone. What do prophets know?
Leave your boat to its straining at the mooring
prow toward Ilium. Let the north wind blow.
Turn your back on the taffrail and on Troy
and walk away with the gale behind you—inland.
Take the course that the *wind* advises: Go.

Epithets

Maybe Athena hated her grey eyes,
and Menelaus wanted hair
the color of a raven's wing.
Maybe the things that others publicize
in you are your own worst despair,
and what they praise the very thing
you'd alter. Someone may become a name
for always roving as a master
mariner, yet deprecate
his restlessness and long to be quite tame
and tranquil, and not chase disasters
others know and celebrate
and blazon to the wide world all the same,
like hair the color of a smoldering flame.

My Mother's Cane

I notice (if I sit with her an hour)
the knobs and gnarlings in the polished wood,
the bumps—what once were twigs—in the blackthorn grain.

Does the wood remember it used to send out buds
this time of year, and does it feel an aching,
every April, in its hardened veins?

Maybe the memory of leaf and flower,
lissomeness and blossoming and bloom,
would swell the withered cells with too much pain.

But maundering on about it—what's the good?
It stays there in the corner of her room;
the wood is dead, and a cane is just a cane.

About the Rain

Yesterday you were right about the rain;
it didn't come. It happens without fail:
I'm always calling for a hurricane—
collecting wet disaster in a pail
even before it has a chance to fall;

I'm mopping up the brook before it rises,
hearing a gutter that hasn't gurgled yet;
and, sodden with foreboding, flood, and crisis,
I'm the only one to be all wet.
But blue sky doesn't comfort me at all:

The leaky world is never watertight,
and with all the future left to plug and seal,
better to be Cassandra and be right
about the rain—it might as well be real.

Annunciations, Nowadays

She didn't expect to be entertaining an angel.
She didn't think: I'll wear the blue sateen
and sit and wait with some needlework or a book—

oh, and another thing; the furniture.
There wasn't a polished prie-dieu, or credenza,
or inlaid table under a mullioned window—

and when it happens, it's much the same with me.
I wish I could say I hear a rush of wings
or I have a little warning, but I don't,

and it's more than likely I'm, like her, in blue—
in weekday jeans, the habit of the morning,
hemmed around by desk and sink and stove.

That's the way it is with so-called angels
nowadays. They still come unannounced,
to a shabby room. But they don't deliver news.

There isn't a message; just a visitation:
A sudden happiness—so unheralded,
so born from nothing, it's not the stuff of daylight

or any logical agency. And though
I can't exactly explain it as an angel,
it's much the same, and I know it when it comes.

Third Person

Sometimes I turn myself from flesh to fiction,
becoming a character seen (in my head)
from a story's point of view, by an omniscient
writer—from outside me, where I picture
I and *me* as *she* and *her* instead.

Mostly, living inside my own first-person
mind is the perspective I prefer;
it's hard enough to make my biased version
true to the protagonist, and—worse—
I might not find enough to like in her.

II :: Happy, He Who
  Knows the Country Gods

Roof-Walker

He leans on the sky up there, as if he's painting
not so much the rust-streaked silver roof
as the shed, the field, the sun—the whole July—
with strokes of barn-red, hay-green, sky-blue air.
Maybe the scene's so blazing-summer dry
you wonder about the reason for the rust;
but think of the Januaries that he's there
sweeping a white mass over the eaves below.
And wonder, then, if you could get accustomed
(up there between the silver or the snow
and heaven) to the roof and to the sky,
to brushing the weather away—and if you'd grow
too seasoned in the barn-roof point of view
to come back down to the flat brown earth you knew.

Snow Devils

Inches beyond the window, the wind comes whirling
upward spirals of white so delicate
they're less like eddies spun in surface—snow
than ballets, pirouette on pirouette:
I'm dazzled—lifted—whirled above myself
till *I'm* the choreographer of winter
who tells the wind to rise, the sun to set—
directs the stars to skate across the sky
on a black transparent lake; till I forget
how it's the sky that holds the world together,
keeping the woods and fields and mountains in;
how it's the window pane that keeps December
out; how it's the body's radiant skin
that veils the body's workings just below
in their complicated dance. I won't remember
how, like the pane of glass, the flesh is thin.

Domain

The pasture's green to the woods, and the mountains
rise from the low hills to the dome of day,
and the green and blue and obliging world is mine—
except for the pond, where the angle of the sun
or the wind, wrong-headed, keeps the water gray.

Easy to *tell* a pasture pond: Be blue.
But think of Canute. The housecarls took his throne
down to the beach and lodged it in the sand
so the king could manage the ocean—and he tried.
The water had ideas of its own.

If Solomon owned this field, he could command
Tharshish and all the navy there to bring
ivory, apes and peacocks, gold and spices
home to him here from the edges of the world.
But there's no pond that listens to a king.

Tapping the Northfield Maples

You have to own the weather along with the maples:
A good word for uncertainty is March,
when everything depends on being able
to keep the air behaving. So you watch—
counting on spring to send the thin sap spilling
into a three-week spell of warm and cold
that guarantees the watery stuff distilling
down into flasks and jugs of thicker gold.
But the problem's not in the nights that have to freeze
or the daytime thaws. It's not in the buckets' filling.
It's not in whether the sap is fast or slow—
the problem isn't even in the trees.
The problem's *wanting*—never being willing
to let the weather and the maples go.

Happy, He Who Knows the Country Gods

fortunatus et ille deos qui novit agrestis
Georgics II, l. 493

There was a time when—far enough from town—
at night the fox would lift his head, uneasy;
at noon a man would stop, lean on his ax
and look around for the laughing in the trees.

Sometimes, now, when I'm walking in the woods,
I see two leaves like the pricked ears of a faun
and stop, and rub my eyes, and drink some water
and hear the drone of the highway, and walk on.

Argument

Let him keep on listing
reasons I should stay;
let him give me logic—
I'll debate the thing all day.

But let him take to pleading
another kind of case,
tearing messy reasons
from his heart—no; that's a place

I won't approach or enter—
where there's not a word to say
or any way to answer.
I can only walk away.

Aphrodite Lifts Aeneas, Wounded by Diomedes

Maybe I should have listened when my father
read how Aphrodite was unmanned—
how Diomedes, when he saw her gather
Aeneas in her arms, struck at her hand
so roughly that she let him fall, her valor
failing her.
  All daintiness and pallor,
off she wailed to Zeus, who only smiled
and touched her white hand, healing it, and said
(just as my father would have), "Silly child!
Go back to Cyprus. Save the tears you shed
and set them as jewels—little drops of joy.
No wonder you're here whimpering! You, at Troy!"
But he was wrong: Her tender hand was sore?
—Aphrodite's is still the harder war.

Jealousy

J'en ai froid dans le coeur.
—Edith Piaf

If it's a monster, it's nothing to joke about.
And it's certainly nothing with pretty emerald eyes.
It's a splinter of ice, and it's colorless, like doubt.
It melts, refreezes, tells the truth and lies.

Faith moves mountains. What about suspicion?
It's a pathetic, gutless thing. To stir
my little mind, it needs the eyes and flesh and
yellow hair of someone else — of her:

She was the one you stayed with when the frozen
highways made it dangerous to come home —
or was she? Am I paranoid, supposing
she was the one you came, this morning, from?

It's a chill that sits on the heart: Until you're sure,
it never reaches body temperature.

The Hyacinth Macaws

Are you thinking about the hyacinth macaws?
Have they flown you away to a riotous Amazon?
No, it's another kind of beak and claws
that's carried you off. I know the place you've gone:
Some day, when she's beside you at the zoo,
you'll hardly hear her nattering on at you
to notice the creatures' bright Brazilian blue;
think of me when she does the things I do.
Think of me when she pulls a net of love
over your cage—between you and a sky
as blue as a strange blue bird. Oh, I can see
it's not the blue macaws you're thinking of.
But next time, when you get the urge to fly,
then, when she's wild to keep you, think of me.

London Zoo

IV :: Flight

Flight

Explain again what lets a swallow fly.
I've heard it all—the principles of flight—
how shape and speed and simple flow of air
can keep a hawk or heron coasting there:
It's not enough. There must be something else
(beyond two dumb wings paddling at the sky)
that lifts the eagle into empty height;
something at work before the first bird flew—
before the silly clanking pterosaur,
before the worm and weed were there, before
the heavy world was hanging in the blue;
so tell me again what agency propels
the starlings through the sky—what other thing;
what trick of physics, what third hidden wing—
what force that doesn't let the sparrow fall,
without which there would be no bird at all.

Gray Bird

What was the bird up there? Whistling and flying
out of a mass of green leaf, down he came.

Gray bird: It should have been enough to look—
to call him clever-eyed and white and gray.
Was he any more a nuthatch for the name
of nuthatch? Did I, by identifying,
see him better?
                          When I found the book
and got him into a syllable or two—
as if to know him all I had to do
was give him a name—the bird had flown away.

Angelica and Benedetta

His best two wines he named for his two daughters.
These grapes grow like his ordinary ones:
They drink the warm earth with a little water—
ripen under the same indulgent suns.
The difference isn't the harvesting or pressing.
It's bred in the vine—the grapes are not the same.
And then, these two are heavy with the blessing
he conferred on each one with its name.

With a name he poured the sky into a thing
sprung from the earth; with a name he makes it sing
in the throat with all the music that attends
a starry angel: On its name—which clings
to the grape from the instant of its christening—
the wine's identity in part depends.

Fattoria San Donato

A Simple Thing

A branch that broke with the weight of the winter snow
went on with April, blooming anyway,
its death not having reached its hasty bud.
How simple—not to stop or think or know;
to answer a single impulse with a drive
that assumes the sap as a habit in the blood;
to carry on with the business of the day
and eat the light and call itself alive.

Running on Desire

A man could rest on what he's done,
saying he's owned and loved and seen
enough to let him lie around
content in the October sun,
except that a man's the odd machine
that runs on what he hasn't found.

V :: The Blue Dogs of Scylla

The Twelfth Labor:
What Eurystheus Sent Back

Say a man, at your behest,
would beat his brawny way to hell
and back again: You might request
a small bouquet of asphodel.

Suppose a posy seems too bland;
suppose your hero has the ear
of Hades: Do you then demand
Cerberus as a souvenir?

When a wish comes back to haunt
the wisher—when the thing you lack
is not a thing you really want,
it's best if you can send it back.

Happiness

You think of it as a summer that's somewhere else,
where the insects are rubies and emeralds in the trees,
flitting through hymns you'll be able to hear—tomorrow,
where petals quiver out on the air like flames.
And plumed birds flash around it, scarlet peacocks
waiting there, tricked out for your arrival:
Music and beauty; that's what you want from it.

What it is is the opposite of that.
It's here already, here in your local April—
what did you picture? A bauble from the sun?
A star come down and planted in a garden
(up the road) and even at noon the dew
hanging like beads of heaven on its leaves?
No. It's more like burdock, say, or vetch.

You want it to be the color of sherbet; strange;
a tulip in blue or melons with violet flesh,
or a tree with arpeggios where the fruit should be,
tended by gods who amuse you while you eat—
who fan it with gold-hinged wings and delicious antics;
sweeter, really, than you can believe. Instead,
it's plain—it's too plain even to be noticed,
as plain as the grass you're walking in today.

Due Diligence

When Hamlet plans a big step — parricide,
it seems quite natural that he won't commit
himself to any action till he's tried
to scrutinize to its roots every bit
of data — past fact, also possible
new fallout; yet we fault him!
                              Don't we let
feared consequence make cowards of us all —
dither and agonize and weigh each pro
and con each balance sheet?
                              Still, say we crawl,
inching, out each branch and test its tip:
From next year's shoots, scarcely in embryo,
spring hydras of new ends through which to slip.
Hamlet, go examine your tomorrows;
what about your yet-unfathered sorrows?

The Tea

At the Cassatt exhibit a machine
allows museumgoers to repaint
the pictures on a small computer screen.
So many options! Hardly a constraint—

in fact, you're almost infinitely able:
Raise a teacup from a lady's knee,
or make her drink—or even move the table.
Charged with every possibility

of wallpaper—decisions that Cassatt
didn't have to make, because the wall
was there and pink and striped, and that was that—
you have the chance to reconsider all

parameters. The pink you thought was fixed
forever on the canvas? Make it blue.
The oils are that easily un-mixed
and mixed again. Such power to undo!

I've made my bed; I lie on it. But why?
What's to prevent me? I could rearrange
everything, my existence, with blue sky
my only limit, piling change on change—

they're terrifying, all the roads not taken
but that could be. Spare us so much voice,
and spare the ones so easily forsaken
under the tyranny of too much choice.

Fire

I'd like to get a flame to weave
reliably around a log,
as neatly as a young retriever
jumps and fetches — holds a stick —
docile, like a well-schooled dog.

I'd like the fire to answer fast
when I command. I'd like the flame
to jump and fetch and know its master —
then, when once it starts to lick
the wood, to be not only tame
but steady, neither blaze nor flicker:

Watch the bounding dog, however!
No two leaps are quite the same.

Flogging the Hellespont

as told by Herodotus

Bivouacked at the Hellespont, the Persians
watched the breakers hit the bridge
and shiver it with the surge,
and Xerxes—purple, shuddering with fury—
sentenced the overweening sea
three-hundred lashes of a scourge:

"Bind it with manacles! Let down chains and fetters
into the insolent waves.
Get the branding iron—stamp the arrogant
billows as my slaves."

Be Xerxes. Break your wrist flogging the ocean.
Curse the sun for insubordination.
And then go out and build the bridge again
and beat your Spartans at Thermopylae.

The Pirates

according to Plutarch

They carved up all the Roman seas
while Rome was off at other wars,
and then they cast their eyes and anchors
at the ports that lined the shores.
And after they'd cut a swath of slaughter,
you could see their ships sashay
superb across the sapphire water,
swanning in glory around the bay:

More than the ravaged Roman islands,
more than the silk in plundered bales,
the murdered girls, the rape and violence,
it was the pirates' purple sails
that brought out Pompey to deliver
the Roman towns—and from the crime
that the pirates' flashing oars were silver
and their gilded masts sublime.

In Posse

Everything about this dress is right,
or could be, if I had a twenty-four—
inch waist. But no. I'm several inches more,
and the belt and hips have always been too tight.

Why do I keep it then? I'll tell you why:
I may be, at the moment, what you see;
inside me is a waist of twenty-three
so real, so in my reach that—*what am I?*
My current size, or the several inches less
that waits there, beautiful and out of view?

The self that slips like silk into a dress!
If you only have it in you, is it you?
If it's there, unexercised? I'd argue yes;
you're what you could—yes, though you never—do.

Regret

Now, in the last few days before the maples
open their yellow-knuckled fists
and take the air in green hands — it's the day
they've dreamed about — and bring an end to April,
straining their elbows, arms and wrists
and every hour closing in on May;

now, with their fingers not quite open yet,
before their thickening green arcade
comes shouldering April away, already I
see in the green a shadow — a regret
that, gaining these few yards of shade,
we lose a mile of cold blue open sky.

Autumn Afternoon

Okay, we're sitting here together
in the same September weather.
I'd call this a chilly spot,
but look at you: You're sweating hot—
which means the single world we share
is two worlds that we can't compare
at all. I get a shivery—
a bloodless—kind of chill, to be
so insulated by a skin
that no one else can travel in.

So far apart, although you're sitting there
inches away; and if two bodies find
such different weather in the common air,
think of the space dividing mind from mind.

The Heat

The heat got into the house, despite the windows
battened down and the heavy curtains pulled
the minute the thick sun shouldered past the willow
to hound the short night's coolness out of morning—
the cool that was nothing more than darker heat
hardly less hot than the day before.

Sunday the thunder came, and the sudden air
scoured chilly channels across the kitchen—
in at the northern windows above the sink
and out again at the windows on the south:
The napkins and newspapers hustled off the table;
soon the house was sixty-five degrees.

But we found the heat on Monday, lying low,
locked away in the closets and a cupboard—
and opened our arms to it, stroked it on our hands;
like a man who's been a month at an icy pole,
who holds with his eyes the new red morning sun
and remembers the heat like a ruby because it's gone.

Iron Pants

New, they were black. Now, top-fuzzed, like charcoal
warming, which a frost-white bloom will dim,
they're still quite thick, a quarter-inch of wool,
but each decade a thought looser on him—
the working "iron pants" my father wore
in winter.
　　　　Summers, on a terrace wall
near the beach, he keeps a large outdoor
thermometer, suspended from a pole
on a four-foot twine—to fish for a temperature
(while standing dry-shod) warm enough to swim.
The shallow water, restless, shingle-turned,
into which July's hot sun is churned,
changes first—a permeable façade.
Well below the surface, his is more
a winter warmth, that underneath the hoar
frost's rime-skin, wears like iron—warms the blood.

Closing

When they sold a farm, along with a deed and witness,
they used to bring a handful of dirt to the table
and thunk it down on a cloth to close the deal.
They didn't need that inch or two of earth
to certify that the land was arable;
and it didn't vouch for more than a single field—
one pile of humus. So, what was it worth?

Not much, but I'd prefer the dirt to *this:*
Signatures, mortgages, notaries, lawyers, liens,
the covenants on the property being sold—
what do they have to do with a piece of land?
Passing papers—nothing's here to hold.

The dirt would show what the transaction means.
An earnest of the farm it's taken from,
the purchaser could weigh it in his hand.
Not much; but then a little heap of loam
is an amount I ought to understand
with the odd affinity I feel for home.

Randolph, Vermont

The Blue Dogs of Scylla

caeruleis canibus resonantia saxa
Aeneid, III

As soon as I've left the reefs behind
and the thrashing straits, and when I've found
my sea legs, when I've caught the wind
and penned the flapping sails around it—
taken the whole wet shaggy air
and brought it to heel and got the waves
to lie down at my dry feet—then
I hear the yelping from the caves
behind me, where the rocks resound
again with the ocean—kennels' baying,
howling me back to them again
as if I'd never been away:
It's memory; it's back there, playing;
the sea-whelps leap in the grotto there—
the foam-white tongues and the old green claws
tear at my ankles with their spray
and take me back in their dark blue jaws.

VI :: Reading the Aeneid

Seeing Carthage

All that remains of Carthage is the sky—
this indigo, indelible as if
Dido brought the blue with her from Tyre
and built a dome for the city with the dye:
That isn't Carthage, spread below us there
in lumps of dun sand dead by the sleeping sea.
The white and purple Carthage Dido knew
under this pantheon of sapphire-vaulted
air—it's gone; it's somewhere else—a poem.
Down there, the Romans plowed the soil with salt.
Nothing remained of Carthage after Rome.

But Carthage is more than the city Scipio wept;
it's the blue song Dido painted overhead.
Things that matter cannot be destroyed,
and those dun lumps were built again with words
into another Carthage—one we've read.
Forget the site down there; the words have kept
the ruined city so alive that, dead,
Dido is even more alive than I am.
She's not here in Sidi-bou-Saïd;
she's closer, poised on a scaffolding in air
painting the only Carthage that we need.

Sidi-bou-Saïd, Tunisia

Leave-Taking

frondentisque ferunt remos et robora silvis
infabricata fugae studio
Aeneid IV 399–400

Up they leap at word they're leaving Carthage,
having dawdled too long on the shores
—the harbor hot, the Punic girls too thin—
and rush to the woods to finish cutting oars.
Dido on the high walls hears them shouting,
sees the treetops thrash—a leafy ocean
calm again when the hot crew, bursting out,
brings from the grove their thick cloud of commotion.

They hack at the raw green oars; but they're for sailing
now, before they're ready—rowing rough,
foiled by the blades with little leaves still trailing
green in the jumping waves when they push off.
Should we tell them, *Wait*? Should we tell them, *Trim the oarshafts*?
No! When the oars are done, there'll only be
something else—some mess, some woman wailing—
to keep them back from the somersaulting sea.

These Same Beasts

Sed tamen idem olim curru succedere sueti
quadripedes et frena jugo concordia ferre:
spes et pacis.
Aeneid III, 541–3

In sight of Italy, Aeneas
read the portent on the shore—
a heavy omen: Four white horses
armor-clad as if for war.

These same horses, nonetheless—
these are the beasts who take the bit
in their soft and willing mouths, who bow
their necks to the yoke and who, submitting
shoulders to the shaft—allowing
back and chest to bend in harness—
break the new ground to the plow.

VII :: Coda

Avogadro's Number

Avogadro knew how many atoms
whirl in a dozen grams of carbon-12.
To understand that hidden spinning dance—
that's to define the universe itself,
elements, molecules, ions, earth and air
brought down to strings of zeroes he could see
as close as if he held them in his hands—
but Avogadro doesn't speak to me.

Tell me the music the guitars would play
in El Dorado. Tell me how its rivers
leap with an ore that imitates the sun—
but not how much the sunburnt ore will weigh.
Enough of numbers. It's a mistake to know
how many light-years to the nearest star—
how great the distance is to El Dorado—
I'll set out, but don't tell me how far.

Personent Hodie

Personent hodie voces puerulae . . .
—Christmas hymn, XIIIth c.

There's a medieval carol that belongs
to boys; it never was a song for men
—who plow through hymns with voices ten-ox-strong—
but boys, who sing it once or twice and then,
Christmas gone, the choir and the songs
are quiet . . . Until January, when,

on Sundays, indoor soccer games replace
the Holsteins at the fairground. Soccer noises
jar the Cattle Building; parents bray,
buzzers reverberate, a coach rejoices,
boards and bleachers bang, balls ricochet,
and everything is discord; but the boys,
weaving, blocking, scoring, also raise
—in patter passed from boy to boy—their voices.

Just this September, the shire horses drilled
in this arena. Here, the bulls and cows
waited beside the big slow Belgians thilled
and yoked as if to pull a painted plow
out of a book of hours—where they tilled
a harder field than this, resounding now

with boys whose descants echo from the roofs—
whose shouts and flickering footwork will be gone
as quickly as the teams of heavy hooves
that plodded autumn—gone with the plows once drawn
in springtime into long medieval grooves
by Clydesdales and by quiet Percherons:
Eight-year-olds, they move the way time moves
and change as quickly as their antiphons.

The Litany of Loreto (Mozart)

The music begins, and you're listening along
when a phrase, or one note, catches you off guard.
Instead of the nice line you'd anticipated,
it swerved away and—rising, falling—jarred
the melody into your mind. Because it's *wrong!*
It's not the pleasant sound it should have been.
But you wait to hear it again—expect it, listen
again, till you grow attuned to it, again—
don't get used to it. Let it stay resistant,
like the idiosyncrasy in a smile
or the jut of a jaw or the rasp in a voice; await it;
keep it asking you to reconcile
something you can't quite get accustomed to:
Love is the work the listener has to do.

Nocturne for Flute

A nocturne that I've never heard before—
and the world comes pouring through the air, expressed
in such bright filaments of liquid sound
that now I wonder: What about the rest?

What other nocturnes are there, and what other
flautists, that I haven't heard of yet?
What other lovers never known or loved?
What friends or colleagues—mentors—never met?

And if it took this long—until tonight—
for me to know a nocturne can exist
like this one, now I listen, half my mind
in mourning for the music I'll have missed.

Soleares Gitanas

to guitarist Manitas de Plata

Yours is a song of solitude and mountains,
as ragged as the rocks and passes where
it goes on feet as dusty as the ground and
twists away—a song that turns to air
(like smoke from sunburnt fires in the narrow
foothill corridors, where no one finds
the fire or the camp) or, when we follow,
mounts a donkey.
     We can walk behind it,
into barren country where your cry
mines the stony desert, and your hands
quarry silver from the desert stone.
But your lament, when once we understand it,
rides away without us—as alone
as if its coda is the empty sky.

Deborah Warren was born in Boston and educated at Harvard. After fifteen years teaching Latin and English, and ten years as a software engineer, she and her husband now raise heifers on a farm in Vermont while living in Andover, Massachusetts. Ms. Warren's work has been published in a great many magazines, including the *Hudson Review*, *The New Criterion*, the *Paris Review*, and the *Yale Review*. She has received the *Robert Penn Warren Prize*, the *Howard Nemerov Sonnet Award*, and the *Robert Frost Award*.

The New Criterion is recognized as one of the foremost contemporary venues for poetry with a regard for traditional meter and form. The magazine was thus an early leader in that poetic renaissance that has come to be called the New Formalism. Building upon its commitment to serious poetry, *The New Criterion* in 2000 established an annual prize, which carries an award of $3000. Deborah Warren is the fourth winner.